Blackened White
Writings by
Brian W. Foster

Table of Contents

Acknowledgements

I could fill an entire book with names and stories of people who have helped me stay alive and thriving, even in recent years, but I want to keep this pertaining to those who had a significant hand in helping this book go from scribbling's and journals, hard drives, iPad's and many, many conversations over coffee and cigarettes at the North Hollywood Diner, to what it is today.

To my parents, Randy and Charlotte: Thank you for throwing your time, money (what little there was of it growing up), love, and grace into my passions, and for never discouraging my creativity but walking alongside me through any portal by which that could flow.

To my sisters, Anita Lorene and Cynthia Ann: You are the sustaining joy of my life and a consistent reminder of the power that family has to heal.

To Brady McGowan: There is literally not one person in Los Angeles whom I have spent more time talking with than you, sir. Thank you for your patience with me. Thank you for always looking at the big picture, and for asking me questions, the most humbling and generous being "What can I do to help?". In this, the world sees your character.

To David and Anita Ruis, the Harrison family, the Scoggins family, and my entire Basileia family: In this world there are dreamers, then there are doers. Thank you for being a family of doers, and for standing by me through the most exhilarating and frightening years of my life.

To Jason Upton: Thank you for never, ever holding back. Thank you for your consistent smile and encouragement, and the hunger you have for truth in the inner man. Our conversations have always left me with something to think and to write about.

To Kevin Max: You truly are a brother. Thank you for never being anyone other than Kevin Max. Thank you for the love and truth you've shown me for so many years, and for writing, singing, and never being afraid of a damned thing.

To Mr. and Mrs. Echols: Thank you for your incredibly generous gift, and the reasons behind giving it. Thank you for believing in me.

And finally, to Troy Baker: Brother, this book would most certainly not exist if it weren't for you. Thank you for listening. Thank you for listening beyond the words to the voice, and for consistently tough-loving me into action. Thank you for pushing me further into my humanity to find the strength to believe in myself and to trust, to learn, to grow, and to be still and write. There is no amount of currency or treasure in the world to repay you for the generosity and support you have given me.

Introduction

On May 1, 2008 I moved to Los Angeles to pursue a "career in music". Rather quickly, I found myself reigniting old addictions and began to unravel a complete understanding of the deficiencies of my human sexuality and lack of self-control. They say this city changes people, but I think Hollywood just tugs on whatever is already brewing under the surface, waiting for someone to pull on it like an endless stream of multicolored tissue cascading out of a magician's sleeve. David Milch, perhaps the contemporary writer I admire most, once said "I know I am about to hit rock bottom when my circumstances are deteriorating faster than I am able to lower my standards". For myself (and those in my immediate "sphere of influence"), this couldn't be more true regarding the past 4 years I've spent in Los Angeles. There is a subtle and beautiful irony that this book is releasing on the anniversary of my arrival here.

My friend, what I offer you in this book is not perfection. I have no money for a literary agent, no admired or celebrity status as a writer (as if there really were such a thing), and although people consistently remind me that I have a few famous friends, I have refused to exploit those relationships for the sake of my "career". Maybe that's why we're still friends. If there are any grammatical or punctual errors in this collection (as I'm sure there are many), I hope you will forgive me. Look past my poor English skills and rather stare into the heart of what I am saying,

If you find some of the subject matter offensive, or should you be confused about my faith, morals, or character as a result of what you read here, then that is the perfect place to begin the conversation that matters. I'm not interested in becoming rich through these writings, nor to live in the shadows of writers and poets who have inspired me over the years. This book is nothing if not an "Open House" flier. These are my observations of truth, as seen through the most pure and most convoluted filters I've worn throughout the last 30 years. If my experience can help another person see truth, or to heal in some way, then I am content.

My journey of life, love, and faith has brought me here, to this specific point, and I refuse to strip it of its significance by censorship. It already stands awkwardly naked, this human experience, in its contrast of "Blackened White".

We cannot truly become free until we embrace the reality that we don't have to convince God we are good. We don't have to convince the world we are important. We don't have to compare ourselves to another, or succumb to a life of chronic vertigo from the revolving door that is shame, once we've come face to face with our own human condition. I am no expert in the matter, and I am becoming increasingly aware that there are no experts, merely observers.

Welcome, and please, stay a while.

Brian W. Foster

1. Night Stand

The nightstand is the confession booth of the bedroom.
Whenever I go to someone's house for the first time, I ask if they own a nightstand.
People are astounded by this.
Baffled, in fact.
In years prior, I used to ask to use the restroom within seconds of entering someone's home.
Then I'd rummage through all the drawers and cabinets for opiates.
If they had some, I would steal some.
If they didn't, I would become angry with them.
I've seen a lot of interesting nightstands in my day though.
People keep sacred things inside them:
Books.
Condoms.
Dirty movies.
Letters.
Birthday or Anniversary cards.
Scented lubricants.
Bibles.
Jewelry.
Perhaps even the occasional remains of a loved one or two.
You can tell a lot about a person by what they keep in their nightstand,
but don't be deceived by what you see on top of it.
It's what's inside that counts,
and whenever I go to someone's house for the first time, that's the only landmark
I'm interested in during the tour.
One never fully grows comfortable with seeing a condom sitting on top of a Bible in a drawer though.
I personally do not own a nightstand.
I don't like people knowing such intimate things about me.
I keep nothing in my home that could be used to define me to strangers or friends.
Except razorblades.

I leave them on the coffee table.
People can think whatever they want about the razorblades,
but one thing is certain:
No matter what they believe the blades are sitting there for,
While they're thinking about it...
Nobody's feet will be on my coffee table.

Cloud 9

I woke up this morning and rolled over to make sure she was still asleep.

Sound asleep despite the time on the clock and the chill in the room. Not wanting to wake her, I pulled my arm slowly from beneath her neck and laid her head back on the pillow as it was.

I wondered what she was dreaming of.

This, as she always said, was her most vulnerable state, and I knew better than to tamper with it.

So I sat up quietly and gently pulled the covers to her shoulders and slid off the bed and onto my feet.

They stung on the cold of the wooden floor and I was careful to watch where I stepped.

The light barely peeked its way through the cracks in the giant walls across the courtyard, letting in just enough light to see my way around, but not enough to force a squint.

I picked up the broom and dustpan in the corner and put them in the closet and closed the door quietly.

Sitting down in the windowsill, I lit a cigarette and blew the grey smoke out of the room and into the sky and ran my fingers through my hair as I watched her sleep.

She always hated when I watched her sleep, but for some reason it was the only time I felt close to her.

The walls were down and the wine was digested and the fight was over.

There was only us, and perhaps this is the moment that we loved each other most. There were no words to get us in trouble, no sour glances or misread statements, no computers or phones or house guests to distract us from each other, and no ticking clock telling me it was time to leave and salvage whatever was left of my day.

I flicked the ash out the window and coughed quietly, but it was loud enough to wake her up.

Sitting up slowly, she brushed her hair out of her face with her fingers and rubbed her eyes for a few moments.

"What are you doing?" she asked.

"Smoking", I replied.

"What time is it?"

"Late", I said. "Early."

She made no eye contact. "I thought I told you to leave last night and not come back".

"Yeah", I replied. "I was hoping you wouldn't remember that this morning".

"Did I hear you come in?" she asked.

"Yeah. You threw a candle at me and told me to fuck off".

"Did I hit you?" she asked.

"No, but the candle did", I replied.

"Oh. Well, if you want me to apologize I'm not going to".

"I know", I said. "I didn't come back for an apology".

"Then why did you come back?"

"Because", I said "Sometimes I'm no good at going away".

"Sometimes I wish you were better at it", she said.

"Sometimes I wish you didn't drink so goddam much". I turned my head and looked outside.

She sighed loudly and stood up from the bed and started to walk toward the window. She was wearing only a pair of white shorts and the silver necklace her mother gave her a few years back, and I watched as she covered her breasts with her arm and shivered in the cold air. She stood in front of me and held out her hand.

"Gimme that", she said, motioning for the half-smoked cigarette between my fingers.

I knew better than to argue with a hung over woman in the morning who needed a smoke. I handed it to her and walked across the room to the bed and sat down. She took my place at the window and sat there topless, smoking and looking out at the building across the street.

I sat on the edge of the bed and just stared at her.

"The fuck are you looking at?" she said, without even glancing toward me.

"The best mistake I've ever made", I replied.

She laughed quietly and took another drag of the cigarette, exhaling slowly and looking over to me.

"You know we can't do this forever?" she said.

"I know"

"Then what do you want to do about it?" she asked.

"What would you do about it, if you were sitting where I am right now?" I said.

She looked down at the courtyard six stories below where she sat.

"Push you out the fucking window, probably", she whispered.

"Would that solve all your problems?" I said.

"No, but it would solve all of yours", she replied.

I shook my head and looked down at my bare feet.

She put the cigarette out in the ashtray and walked over the bed and sat down next to me, laying her head on my shoulder and putting her arm through mine. She took my hand, raised it to her face and kissed it gently.

"Come on, let's go downstairs and get breakfast, I'm fucking starving", she said.

"What do we do about what happened last night?" I asked.

"Nothing", she said. "We're over it".

"How do you know we're over it?"

"Because neither one of us ended up in the courtyard with white chalk outlining our bodies", she snapped. "I would call that relational progress."

"Really?" I asked sarcastically.

"Yes, really", she replied. "Now let's go".

I picked my jeans up from the ground and put them on as she put on her torn grey shirt across the room.

"Well", I said. "Close the window before we leave so it isn't bloody freezing in here when we get back".

"Fine", she said walking back over to the window.

She grabbed the window frame from the bottom and pulled it closed quickly, freeing the last few remaining shards of broken glass left in the frame. They fell to her feet and she jumped back in fright and looked over at me.

"What the fuck!" she screamed.

I looked up at her and smiled for a moment, then walked over to the bed and flipped over the pillow that I had slept on.

She stared at the blood for a moment before covering her face with her hands.

"Progress indeed", I said.

Where I am Going, You Can't Take Me

Dearest Victoria,

I wish I could begin this letter with "I don't know why I thought of you tonight", but we both know why. So the years have passed, and I know this letter will find you better than when last we spoke. As for me, every day is a climb, and the only thing keeping me from falling is the view that awaits me at the top of this mountain.

I spoke to someone tonight about you. It's hard not to do when talking about love and loss. You remain my greatest triumph and my greatest failure. It's funny, the complexities we strip once our hearts can reconcile the decisions we've made before we're even able to understand their implications. Perhaps, time is catching up with me. Either way, to say I don't miss you would be a lie, and a disgrace to all we shared. But what is that worth, now? You belong to someone else, and my life has become a series of conscious decisions, which seem to merely keep my head above water, at least long enough to take a breath before the current pulls me under.

I move, yes, but I'm still here. I'm still standing on the corner of 3rd and Broadway, with your hands touching my face, and you're telling me you love me for the first time since we met. I'm still here, laying naked in your bed, listening to the song we've since pretended doesn't exist, our fingers interlaced and our breathing a steady, synchronized rhythm as we shut our eyes and for just that moment, pretended the world was everything we wanted and needed it to be. I'm still here. I'm still on the other end of the phone, listening to you cry as you tell me I can't leave you. I'm still punching holes in the wall of my apartment with one hand, and holding the phone in the other as the tears reach my lips and I try stoically to stand my ground and let you go.

They tell me I'm "not over it". Yes, the time we spent, the love we made, the fights we suffered through and overcame, are all summarized as "it" by the passersby.
You ruined me. I'm not ruined, but you ruined me. I can't forget the

brokenness of your voice when you were afraid, and the strength of your touch as you held me while I clung to life in what could have been my final moments. It was you who brought me back. It was you who brought me here.

I'm still here, and the buildings all look the same, only the tenants have changed. Twenty more paces and I could see the light coming from your window, yet I refuse to walk around that corner. Maybe one day I will, but tonight I'm content to sit here and write to you from just out of reach. Ironic, isn't it?

We both said, "I'm sorry" so many times, I can't remember who was to blame in the first place.

The bottle perhaps. Yes, we'll blame the bottle. It's much easier to blame the product than the consumer.

But you consumed me, and I consumed you until there was nothing left. So don't ever wonder why I'm always empty. I poured myself into you, and that is one thing that cannot be undone. I'm sure if I didn't love you, I would hate you, but hate cannot reside in my blood when the memory of your touch is more tangible to me than the scars on my arms.

I'm still here, tasting the wine on your lips, and seeing the glaze in your eyes when it was time to pry the glass from your fingers and carry you off to bed.

I'm still here staring at the shimmer of the needle on the nightstand and the candle's reflection on the wall of your bedroom.

I know this letter will find you better than when last we spoke.

I'm still here, right where I left you...
...at the bottom of an empty bottle, and the needle is on the nightstand.

-Henry

We're Fine

It's never difficult to remember a time before this
A time when you were the object of my passions
You were the target of my desires
Before the tears, the scowls, the shouting and the running away
When the music played for hours and we were next to each other
When every word we finally spoke to break the minutes of silence
Brought a cry of laughter
A touch, a kiss
Which eclipsed all others
The remembrance of why we keep this alive
And breathing
And moving
Now, I wonder if a stranger was born inside this picture frame
Had a thief come in, stolen your portrait
And replaced it with a water color
Barely recognizable and hardly desirable
But I keep holding on…
Always, just holding on…
Is it hope that drives me?
Or madness?
Is it fear that drives me to your steps in the middle of the night?
When you throw my love down onto the street
Like china through a third story window
They tell me it's a waste of money to keep buying more
To restock the shelves when I get back into the house
To go out before daybreak
And sweep the broken shards from the streets
Never trying to catch them as they fall
Never trying to glue the pieces back together
I only know their worth to me…
…broken, shelved, or served upon

Into the Wind

"Are you ok?"

I must have woken up quickly and shaken the bed, waking her.

"I'm fine. Go back to sleep."

I wiped the sweat from my forehead with my arm. It was cold as ice and a chill ran down my spine as I swung my legs over the side of the bed and rested my feet on the cold floor.

"The dream?" she asked.

"No. I'm fine. Go back to sleep."

She rolled back onto her side and reached her arm behind her, grabbing my hand and holding it for a few moments before the pattern of her breathing settled into a steady rhythm and I knew she had fallen back asleep.

I leaned forward and watched as the silver cross around my neck swung back and forth. I stared at it for a solid minute; almost hoping the hypnosis of the constant motion would help me retire to my dreams once again.

It didn't.

I looked over at the nightstand and squinted in the darkness, trying to sharpen the red numbers on my clock to see what time it was.

I guess it didn't matter. I knew it was late, and I knew the day had officially begun for me.

I stood up and walked over to the sliding glass door and opened it slowly, glancing over my shoulder to make sure I wasn't waking her again.

She had somewhere to be in the morning, I didn't.

She needed her rest, and I knew I wouldn't be resting.

The dream was the same, yes. Perhaps I would learn to not be so afraid of it once I could make sense of it. I stepped out onto the balcony and lit a cigarette. It must have been 100 degrees, in the middle of the night.

I loathe heat, and being in Las Vegas this time of year is like trying to sleep in a dragon's mouth as he's winding up to exhale an entire city into eternity.

Suddenly I remembered something my father told me when I was a

child. He said "Always leave your troubles between the door frame and the bed frame, or you'll never know the meaning of rest".
I guess after all these years; I still haven't quite mastered the art of releasing my fears and failures before attempting to sleep.

She wasn't my wife, and she never will be.
She's a warm body in a cold bed.
Someone to laugh with, someone to care for and provide for. I knew I would never love her like I did the one before her, and part of me believed she knew this too.

She was my opiate now, and the second she fully realized it, I knew she would disappear into the wind.

Maybe I should do the right thing and let the wind take her, but for now I'll just enjoy the breeze against my skin.

Jessica

I hadn't said a single word in half an hour.
My coffee was lukewarm and tasted like a tire iron.
I looked across the table at her, realizing she never liked to make eye contact when she spoke.
So I just stared into her eyes, hoping she'd look up at me and become instantly uncomfortable.

Finally, she stopped talking long enough to take a drag of her long extinguished cigarette.
"Ha...it's out", she said, pointing to the inch and a half of ash resting on the end of her Marlboro.
I tapped my fingers on the table, pinky to index finger in a slow and trailing motion.
"I'll give you $20 to stop talking for 5 minutes", I told her.
"What?" she asked.
"The offer stands", I replied.
"I'll give you $40 to leave", she retorted.
"I invited you here."
"Just because you invited me here doesn't mean I can't stay here without you."
"What are you gonna do if I leave?" I asked her.
"I dunno...eat some cake probably".
"You've got 6 pieces of french toast in front of you that you haven't touched."
"I'm not hungry anymore".

I rubbed my eyes. This conversation was as useful as a broken rubber band.

"I'm leaving", I said as I stood up from the table.
"You don't want to talk to me anymore?"
"We aren't talking...you're talking. I'm examining this spoon, trying to figure out if it's sharp enough to cut my throat."
"Very funny, sit down".
I sat back down.
"What would you like to talk about?" I asked.

"Do you think I'm pretty?" she asked me.

I stood up, walked to the rack and put my hat and coat on.

"Oh come on", she said, waving me back over to the table. "I'm just kidding."

"You owe me $40", I said.

"I don't have $40".

"Hey, the deal was, you either stop talking and I pay you, or I leave and you pay me, either way I come out on the long end of this transaction."

"Fine", she said, taking two $20 bills out of her purse and handing them to me.

"Much obliged", I said as I tipped my hat to her and walked out the door and out to my bicycle.

It wasn't until the next morning when I got carded at the liquor store, that I realized my wallet was gone.

I wondered how she was going to spend the other $200 that was in there.

Guess I'll ask her out to a nicer place for the second date, see if she wants to go Dutch.

Cringe Benefits

There's a woman I don't love
And she's banging on my door
And she wants to be inside of here
So I can be inside of her

But I'm a different man
Than the one I was before
So I tell her through the door
That I think she needs to find another door

Lawton Outlaw Moved to Texas

Lawton Outlaw moved to Texas
I miss him everyday
He used to say things like "I don't like that stuff, dude." and "Nah,
you shouldn't say stuff like that."
Kept me in line, that tattooed bastard did.
Patrick used to do that, but not in the same way.
He was the kind of guy who would yell like he was mad at you for
something he did.
Every man needs a good friend, not a bad father.

All anyone out here cares about is what I can do for them.
Or what they can get from me.
This isn't the city of broken dreams; it's the city of broken people.
And I'm one of them.

Sitting in my car on Ivar
Parked at an out of order meter
Popping pills and washing them down with a Heineken I found
under the backseat
Wiping the tears from my eyes
And wishing my best friend wasn't dead
Searching for any piece of ass drunk enough to compliment my jacket
and ask me directions to The Hotel Cafe.
The truth is, I hate this town, and I think she hates me too.

Blink

Nobody ever accused me of being ahead of my time
Quite the opposite actually
It's often people tell me "You were born in the wrong era" or "You're such an old soul"
Perhaps it's because I've lived nine lives already
But coming back from the dead isn't as exhilarating as you might think
You have to learn how to walk again
How to speak
How to interact with your peers, and with society
You have to settle among the human beings
Find something you can do, and become good at it
So you can feed yourself and stay alive
Long enough to destroy it somehow and start again
You have to find your place in this world
But every time you die and come back to life
The world changes

And I'm sitting here in this cold room
Looking out my window at the blackened white
Trying to make sense of the madness
When my phone rings at 3am
And useless women want me to meet them at a bar on Sunset
So we can drink, do the dance, and then neither of us will need each other again
Until our load gets heavy and whatever we have in front of us isn't enough
But I'm not ready to die again
Not yet

So I stare at Chandler, sitting on the table across the room
The ceiling fan is drying my eyes, and every time I blink
Things get blurrier than the time before
They said of Chandler, "He wrote as if pain, hurt, and life mattered"
I squint my eyes, trying to sharpen the digital red numbers on the box across the room

And for a moment, I imagine her face against my face
My hands brushing against the fabric of her dress as we danced
The taste of the whiskey in my mouth
And the feeling of her skin on my skin
That moment of release when the world turns upside down
Is shaken, and whatever remains in its pockets falls to the floor next to my clothes

Then I'm all alone with the world
And this naked, fragile, and broken soul lying next to me
I know I'll gather my things and leave before she wakes up
It's what I've always done
But I'm not ready to die again
Not yet
So I press "Ignore" on the telephone
Turn off the lamp in the corner
Lock the door
Put my back to it and lean
Close my eyes
In that moment...
I'm alive
Because I know the Thief in the night
And He doesn't call
At least not the way the others do

The Christmas Party

I stepped out of my car and into the street, looking up at the house in front of me before closing my door and examining myself.

My shirt was inside out, and my solid black tie was covered in cigarette ash.

The house was a two-story monstrosity half a mile up Plymouth Ave, and the only thing more frightening than the mathematically aligned barrage of blinking lights, was the dozens of mini-vans, station wagons, and hybrid hatchbacks parked on the street in front of the house.

I brushed the ash off my tie and grabbed my coat from the backseat. The shirt was fine how it was.

As I walked up the brick stairs on my way to the front door, I remembered the invitation I received in the mail the week before. "Calling all friends and Christmas lovers!" read the front of the card, with a picture of my friend and his wife, dressed in the most fluorescent play-doh looking sweaters and scarfs I'd ever seen. It looked like someone put all the Sesame Street puppets in a blender, then knitted the remains together while high on crystal meth and Bing Crosby.

I still can't explain why I called to RSVP. Maybe I'm lonely? Maybe I'm hungry? Maybe I'm neither.

I knocked softly on the front door, almost hoping no one would answer so I could just get back in my car and drive home, armed with the "No one came to the door" excuse for the inevitable phone call I'd receive upon knowledge of my absence. But alas, my hopes and dreams were shattered by my former college roommate's wife pulling open the door with a force I can only compare to Noah, once he realized there was dry land outside the ark.

"You're here!" she screamed.

I turned around briefly to make sure the windows of my vehicle were still intact.

My god, woman, I thought to myself.

She greeted me with an uncomfortably long hug and took my coat immediately.

"Everyone's upstairs", she said. "Make yourself at home".

I forced a smile and "Thank you" as she made her way back into the kitchen. I made slowly for the staircase, looking down at my filthy shoes and hoping no one would ask me to take them off. It was laundry day and I wasn't wearing socks. Not paying detailed attention to my surroundings, I placed my left hand on the side rail, not realizing it was covered in plastic holly and thousands of small, pointy Christmas lights.

Ouch.

Obscenities ensued under my breath as I pulled my hand to my face to examine the damage. No blood, but now I really wanted to leave. What felt like 37 minutes later, I reached the top of the windy staircase and stood, out of breath, before two double doors. I could hear loud music and talking coming from the other side of the doors, and I knew exactly what awaited me behind this protective fortress of solid oak. Nevertheless, I had come this far, there's really no turning back without looking like a supreme asshole. I opened the door and walked in slowly, hoping I wouldn't be greeted in the same fashion as I was when arrived at the house. Thankfully, only a few people noticed me when I walked in, and they had no clue who I was, so they just turned back around and resumed whatever strange activities they were involved in before my slow and painful entrance. Still standing in the doorway, I looked around and saw a few friends, most of whom I've known since I was a kid. They've all grown up, married, and have "successful" careers, children, retirement plans, planned vacations, planned date nights, planned sex nights, planned

taco salad nights.

It was like walking into a color-coded spreadsheet nightmare house.

But I digress...

A couple of familiars noticed me, came over and said hi, "Happy Holidays", "Merry Christmas", etc. I smiled half-assed and mumbled "Likewise", scouring the room with my eyes, hoping to see if Jim Beam had been invited to the party or not. There was no sign of him, or any of his friends for that matter. I was clearly underdressed. Everyone was wearing their Christmas sweaters, much like what was on the front of the hosting couple's invitation I received. They were all smiling, laughing, telling stories about their children, and eating handful after handful of green and red cookies that were shaped like trees, bells, and little angels with trumpets. I avoided the food like the plague, wondering if it may contain some defiling potion that turned normal, everyday people into fiberglass statues of frightening merriment once a year. This is not a chance I was willing to take, my friends. I decided to just observe everyone gorging themselves instead.

As could have been expected, my friend Peter spotted me and made his way across the room toward me, practically skipping with his ridiculous Santa hat on. I watched as the white ball on the end of the hat's curl bobbed up and down with each step he made. I looked at his feet, half expecting some twisty green elves' shoes or the like, but was disappointed when I saw his trademark penny loafers from college.

"You made it?" he said, his voice cracking with glee like a surprised 12 year old who's date actually showed up to the Jr. High ice cream social.

"I guess so", I replied, still looking around the room for some type of relief in the form of liquid courage.

"How is everything?" he asked...still smiling.

"Everything is as it was, my friend", I answered. Sure, I was being short on purpose, but you have to understand that, despite the fact I've known these people most of my life, we have virtually nothing in common.

A pulse, perhaps, and the rest is questionable.

"Well, we're glad you made it. I know you're not the biggest fan of Christmas, but we like to go all out every year in celebration of our Lord's birth", he said.

I looked around the room at all the decorations. There were trees everywhere, giant Santa Claus statues, mistletoe, plastic reindeer, presents, snow wallpaper and holly, dreaded holly all over the place.

"Look", I said, trying not to laugh. "Unless you worship a fat, elderly man with a weird animal fetish that likes to have little kids sit on his lap, I don't think any of this has to do with the celebration of the 'Lord's' birth".

He just stared at me for a solid minute, with the blankest and most vacant look in his eyes. It was as if he had just seen "Schindler's List" in IMAX the day after finding out he was half Jewish.

Suddenly he broke into obnoxious laughter and patted me on the shoulder several times. I just looked down at his hand and back at his face.

"You always were the life of the party, man", he said.

"If you say so", I replied.

"Can I offer you something to drink?" he asked.

Finally, I thought to myself.

"Well, do you have anything of the adult nature nearby?" I said. "I tend to get a bit skittish in situations like these, being the sort of lone ranger that I am. It helps me relax."

"Oh yes, my friend. You're in luck. Tim and Amy brought over some Bailey's! Let me get you a cup of hot coca and throw a bit of the Bailey's in there for ya, that should do it!"

You racist prick, I whispered under my breath as he skipped back toward the snack table. He returned a few moments later with a Jack Frost mug full of hot coca...and not so full of Bailey's. I took a small sip and smiled at him as he just stood there, smiling at me like the guy from those male enhancement commercials.

Yes, that'll be all, I thought to myself. You can go now.

We small chatted for a few more minutes, and a few others eventually made their way over to me. Over the course of an hour or so, I engaged in dozens of trite and melodramatic conversations with these, my "lifelong" friends. We discussed their "holiday plans", their holiday bonuses at work, their children's various sports activities, their children's dieting and sleeping habits, their children's report cards, their children's haircuts, and their college and career plans for their children.

My ears eventually grew tired of listening to this domestic weirdness and my eyes were bloodshot as my head began to pound harder and harder with every one of their child's third grade photographs that was shoved in my face amidst endless inquiries of "When are you going to finally settle down and start a family?" After I had all I could take of this "party", I said my cordial goodbyes and made my way back downstairs and out to my car. I opened my door and took one last glance at the house.

So fully alive, yet so fully dead, I said to myself.

I drove downtown and parked my car on Main street and got out, walking in the cold to my favorite diner for some caffeine and nicotine, hoping to cleanse my brain from spending the last few hours disappointing people with the fact I had no wife, no minivan, and no children to parade around. They were all so cheerful, and all so happy to be celebrating whatever the hell they thought Christmas was, but I just couldn't help but notice it all felt so rehearsed, so contrived. I don't know. I've never been in their shoes so I can't say for certain. All I know is, next year, I'll probably be "out of town" for the holidays.

As I walked past 6th street, I heard a familiar voice coming around the corner. It was the sound of an old man, beating the hell out of a guitar and singing at the top of his lungs.

I stopped momentarily and just listened.

Charles.

I turned around and walked down 6th street to the corner of the next block. There he sat, bundled up in newspaper and filthy sheets, smiling from ear to ear, singing, "Hark the Herald Angles Sing" with his eyes closed and his head pointed at the sky. I'm pretty sure he didn't hit a single correct note with his voice or guitar, but damn if his wasn't the most genuine smile I had seen all night. I stood in front of him for a moment, then took out whatever cash and change was in my pockets and threw it into the empty guitar case in front of him. He stopped playing momentarily, opened his eyes, and smiled again.

"Where you been brotha?" he shouted. "Up-town with the up-tights?"

I smiled and sat down next to him on the sidewalk.

"Don't stop playing on account of me, man". I told him.

He slapped me on the arm and yelled, "Alright, alright, here we go" and started beating his guitar again.

"Lemme tell you 'bout Christmas", he said as he played, closing his eyes and looking up into the night sky with that cunning smile on his face again.

"You know...baby Jesus was homeless when he showed up!" he said.

I laughed for the first time that entire evening, and I just sat there and smiled while my friend sang and told me stories for hours.

Charles was the happiest man I knew...and he didn't own a damned thing.

Chain Coffee

There we sat, McG and I
Outside a chain coffee store which I refuse to name
Because I'd rather have you get your coffee from Peet's

It's like McG always says, "Starbucks knows how to make money,
Peet's knows how to make coffee"

And I'm reading him selections from a book this guy wrote, back
when it meant something to say something

He's sitting across the table from me listening, then starts to tell me
about this dream he had the night before
All I remember him saying was that "the music seemed like it was
coming from nowhere and it all sounded like John Mayer"

I nodded my head every other sentence and finally concluded that
this must have been a nightmare
Feeling bad for him and his dream where John Mayer songs were
coming from nowhere, I changed the subject

Now, there's something you have to know about McG:
He's an artist, but the real kind
These days, we call anyone who can use Photoshop or operate
GarageBand an artist
But McG isn't that kind of faux, he's the real deal
This guy actually believes that we can create something beautiful, and
that the world can be changed as a result
Most people call him naive, but you see I can't survive without this
guy

So we start talking about art, as we usually do
And the cars pass us on Riverside in Burbank
People walk by us, talking into their ear penises and chomping down
on fiber bars
And a woman adjusts her skirt before walking into the Italian
restaurant across the street

We sit at the table, in the shadow of Disney and Warner Bros
In a valley, surrounded by mountains purchased by men of means
decades ago
Just on the north side of the hill from the "creative capital of the
world"
And we read words written by men, back when it meant something to
say something.

Drawn

Fear never drove any man to a God of love.

Robert Downey Jr.

I had a dream last night where my roommate was teaching Robert Downey Jr. how to play the ukulele.

We we're sitting in a corner inside of this two story Mexican restaurant somewhere near downtown Los Angeles

And all of us were so drunk that the restaurant manager had to hang curtains up around the famous people to keep us from bothering them

I walked over to the manager and yelled at him.

"Hey man, that's not nice. My friend just gave Robert Downey Jr. free ukulele lessons at the comfort of his own table while he ate. You think that just because that guy makes moving pictures for a living that he deserves more special treatment than my friends or me? We're eating the same food as they are, paying the same price for the food we're eating as they are, but we are most certainly going to drink more than Robert Downey Jr. and the two guys he brought with him, and everyone else in this bar as a matter of fact."

In order for this story to be factually correct, I must inform you that the majority of the last part of what I said I yelled to the manager was said from the sidewalk, because some huge Mexicans had already thrown me out and Robert Downey Jr. wiped his face at me with a napkin before I left. You know what I mean. He looked up and over at me out of the corner of his eye too, without even moving his head.

It was that kind of face wiping look.
I'm pretty confident that's an insult in some cultures.

I'm also pretty confident that, even though this was just a dream, if I ever see Robert Downey Jr. at a Mexican restaurant, or on the street, or in a bar somewhere, I'm going to tell him he shouldn't bother trying to learn the ukulele because it's not a very sexy instrument and it won't get you laid.

But I would tell him I'm glad he's not doing drugs anymore.

Not that that's any of my business.

The Mourning After

When we finished, I held you for what felt like hours
And I know we fell asleep
Because I watched the sun rise across your back
Inch by inch
The room filled with light
And your skin moved with the warmth
Coming through the window
I traced the light on your body with my fingertips
Your legs moved beneath the sheets
And touched mine
Your hand reached for my face
I heard it scratch against the rough surface of my skin
And you opened your eyes
Lashes brushing against the pillow
The faintest sound in a quiet room
I savored these seconds like years
And knew only a few more remained
Until you fully came to
And said "Who are you?"

Carnival

My chest is itching
The coffee was cold before I got here
My glance switches between the waitress's face and the lack of steam
rising from the cup
She leaves me
Out the window, there's a carnival across the street from the
restaurant
Children screaming at 9pm on a Friday
I was never allowed to ride the Ferris wheel whenever the carnival
came to town
"Those things are held together with wooden nuts and bolts", my
father would say
We'd drive by in the afternoon and see them setting up the rides and
attractions
Then later that night or weekend, I'd walk past the carnival and see
the other kids playing
Some laughing, some crying, some stuffing their mouths with cotton
candy and giant turkey legs and ice cream
But I always paid attention to the attendants
These mid thirties white men in flannel shirts
Chain-smoking
Pieces of grilled cheese sandwiches
Stuck in their steel wool beards
Pulling levers with the blankest looks on their faces
Like they were somewhere else
I guess a paycheck is a paycheck if you're one of them
But that made me not want to ride their rides
Even if my father would have allowed me to
If the people running the damned thing weren't happy to be there
Then something inside me told me I wouldn't be either
I guess that's how I feel when I go to church sometimes.

The Cahuenga Past

Driving down Cahuenga at 7pm on a Friday night can be a son of a bitch
Especially when I'm empty handed because somewhere between my house and Best Buy
I forgot what I was going there to buy in the first place
Probably something I don't really need
But sitting here, smashed between these Prius' and hybrid minivans has me thinking
I'd love to upgrade my current mid-sized suv to a more eco-friendly model
Not because I care about the environment, which I do
But mostly because they're quiet, you can sneak up on people, blind people
Also, you can save money when you're commuting from this dreary location to that one
In this perfectly weathered city of ours, where the creative and the cremated find a common ground:
Neither of us are going anywhere soon

My phone is full of little 160 character messages that people send me
Telling me I don't write enough, don't drink enough, don't go out enough, and swear too much
Maybe it's not because I'm afraid of what's out there, I just like what can happen in here too much
When I let it happen

The other day, someone tells me "Lots of people watch American Idol, millions in fact"
My answer is always "Lots of people believe the earth is 3,000 years old too"
That's usually when the other party informs me their significant other needs them back home
And I always prefer to stay at the diner or coffee shop, watching people work, text, and talk
These people, these Los Angelinos are my people, my tribe, and one day I hope to make enough money off of them

To be able to move far, far away from them and live the rest of my life in a cottage on the countryside,
Chopping my own firewood and smoking tobacco out of a pipe, cranking out the occasional page on my 1947 typewriter
My dad bought me for Christmas last year at a garage sale in Orange County
Don't even get me started on Orange County
I once had to commute there when I worked for a construction company, and now I feel I can't give "The OC" the shit it deserves
Because my mother lives down there, and I have this sort of code in regards to bagging on places in which my mother resides
Call me old school

So I'm sitting here, staring at young adults on billboards who haven't eaten in weeks, and probably got paid as much to model
As the Photoshop artists who touch them up afterwards and make them look as good as they do now
And all I can think about is giving them a hug, and inviting them over for a 40 of Oxy and a bottle of Shaw
But perhaps that's what brought us here in the first place, so maybe it's not a good idea
The truth is I was born here, but I wasn't raised here, and now I'm back here
And I may not be working the ground, but I'm not networking around and trying to find my place in the world
I know where it is, and if I'm not there yet, there's no one to blame but myself
But I'll tell you this much, I'm sure as hell not passed out on the floor of some studio apartment
In small town northern California with a needle sticking out of my arm, holding a photograph of the love of my life
And telling all the passersby "I wish things could have been different"

Now that I think about it, I don't think I'll buy a hybrid
Not because I don't care about the environment, which I do
But because I like this car
Sure, it's banged up, run down, and has cost me a fortune to fix time

and time again

But every accident I've been in, every time I've had to fork out $300 here or $1,400 there has woken me up

And made me feel alive, even if it was a result of fear or worry or being broke and frustrated

And wanting to give up

The truth is I never have, and I never will

And if I can say anything to the 3 people reading the nothing that this something is

I'm saying to hold onto what you have, even if it's broken and bruised, shattered and ruined

Because maybe, just maybe, the thing you hold has the same affections for you

Fear is a Poison

Fear is a poison
Like blood in the ocean
And our insecurities scream

Love throws all our dreams
Down onto the street
Where the beggars and millionaires meet

Where lies get exchanged
And faces are changed
To make us who we want to be

But truth is a vagrant
A wandering pagan
Its seekers a long, dying breed

And my heart cannot beat
When it's under your feet
And you've run till your legs have grown weak

So I'll go find the home
Where your love is now enthroned
For the anchor you've severed is free.

The Hotel Figueroa

She only knocked once
Maybe that was her calling card
Nobody ever knocks only once
And there's always that moment
Where I'm sitting on the corner of the bed
Television off, phone off
Tilting my head to the left
Trying to figure out if it was a knock I heard
Or just my nerves playing tricks on me

Another single knock
This time I was sure of it

I walked over to the door, unlatched the chain
And led her in

She took off her coat, throwing it and her huge purse onto the floor
It wasn't my place, so I didn't care if she made a mess
She knew this

"You know", came the first words. "It's cheaper if we stay outside of town."
"It's cheaper if we stay out of each other's lives".
She laughed. "Cheaper for you, maybe."

I sat there, hands on my knees. "Anyways."
She sat down next to me, "Anyways."
"Is that a new necklace?" I asked her.
"Really?" she blinked once, her glance moving across the room with
an aggravated slowness until she was looking me in the eye.
"Yeah, never mind."

We never made it into the sheets, and I suppose I understand why
people say never to touch the bedspread.

Afterwards, she lit a cigarette and flicked the ash into one of the paper coffee cups on the nightstand.

"Can you smoke in here?" I asked her.

"I can", she exhaled, handing the cigarette to me.

I took a couple drags, then a few sips of the Jameson bottle from the mini bar.

"Find something on television for us to watch", she whispered, laying her head on me, as her fingers scrolled across my chest. "I have an hour."

I took the television remote out of the drawer and turned it on, flipping through the channels one by one as I finished the cigarette.

"Where's your girlfriend tonight?" she asked.

"Out drinking", I replied.

She smiled, "Hmm, sounds like somebody has trust issues."

"Yeah, somebody does."

Johnny

"Fucking you would be a mistake, and I'm fully aware of that every time I dial your phone number.

Your business card gave me a paper cut when I pulled it out of my coat pocket.

That was the only sign I passed on my way to you, and I should have just rolled a cigarette with it and put a Band-Aid on my finger.

Putting my lips on my own blood is something desperate women do in movies, and I'm proud enough to say I'm above it.

You never cross my mind until I've had more to drink than I've had to eat.

That should tell you all you need to know about my emotional involvement in this situation, so why don't you just stop asking and either agree to these terms or go about your business and never contact me again."

It truly was the longest email she'd ever sent me.

Peace Be With You

We got rained in on our anniversary
I watched the pope make a speech on television.
I put the magazine I was holding up to my eyes, so the captions were covered up
then I muted the television.
I wanted to see if I could make out what he was saying based solely on the level of emotion I saw him express.
With his lips.
With his hands, his facial gestures.
The way he shifted on the podium.
The way his eyes looked into the crowd of devotees before him.
How fast he blinked.
The way he turned the pages of his speech in front of him, and how often he looked down to the words on those pages.

When I woke up, she was asleep, and the dog had chewed up the magazine.

Letterman's on.

In the Beginning

Some would say it started in sin
But I believe it was providence
Perhaps naivety is my blindfold

When the headlights approached
My heart pounded and I turned the music down
Lit a cigarette
And watched you walking up the hill in my rear view mirror
Knowing it was dark enough for you not to notice

I remember the sound of your shoes on the pavement
The way you pushed your hair behind your ears
And even though you couldn't see me
I saw the smile brush across your face, as you were just a few feet
away

When the door shut
When I tasted the whiskey on your lips
When you crawled on top of me and pulled at the buttons on my shirt
When the night turned to morning
And the sun crawled up to the windshield and knocked

My hand, rested on your leg
Your head, rested on my shoulder

The smell of sweat and passion...
Alcohol and abandon...
Some would say it started in sin

The only thing longer than the drive home
Was the drive back to you the next night
And the next night
And the next

And even though it wasn't just right
It was the perfect way

It was the only way
And it will always be the way we began

Now, every time I look over at you as we drive
I remember those January nights
Your legs wrapped around me
Grasping for air as we left the earth
Just for those moments

We came
Then we came back down

If it was heaven we touched
Then my heart longs for home
More than it ever has
And ever will

Shipwrecked

We were shipwrecked

The cabins flooded in seconds
And the fire danced on top of the water
As if to say "not all who surface will survive"

I followed the anchor to the air
And I searched for you
But you weren't there

Arm over arm
Foot crossed over foot
I closed my eyes, breathed full
And sank

Palm to forearm
I pulled and pulled
Until I felt the water break above us
And I heard you breathing

I collapsed and fell below
All of my strength dissolved
And felt the water fill my lungs
Burning and weighing and pulling me into the dark

Palm to forearm
You pulled and pulled
Until we reached the shore

Mouth to mouth
You breathed
Fist to chest
You pounded
Until I was revived
And awoke

I couldn't tell the water on my face
From your tears

"You wouldn't let me die"

Stay

It was one of those mornings where I wasn't sure if she was here or
not
I rolled over onto my side and reached for her
Nothing
I looked to my left
the muscles in my neck tightened
confirming I was in fact, awake
I heard her speak before I noticed her eyes were already open
"Hey"
The crackling in her voice brought a smile to my face
"Hey"
She rubbed her eyes and brought her arm to my chest
Moved her leg in between mine

And in that moment, when her skin touched my skin
I knew I wouldn't be going back to sleep

"Come here", she whispered
"I'm here"
"No, come closer"

I slid closer to her on the bed, pressed her hand against my chest and
breathed
In the silence, I prayed
And thought about what obstacle I must overcome, what depth of
death I must achieve
To be able to stay here, forever
Then I see the smile peer across her face from beneath her hair
She reached up and kissed me
I pressed her leg against my legs
And stared up at the ceiling fan
Watching it shake as it circled

"Do you want to rob a bank today?" she asked.
"For the money, or for the rush?" I replied.
"We don't need the money."

"Would you love me if I was poor?" I asked.
"You are poor."
She got up from the bed, covered her breasts with her arm
and walked over to her clothes in the corner.
"Ok...poorer?" I corrected.
She smiled, put her shirt on and walked back over to the bed and
stood next to where I was laying.
She looked down at me and ran her fingers through my hair,
then walked over to the desk and picked up my typewriter and a half
empty pack of cigarettes.
"What are you gonna do with those?" I asked.
She set the typewriter down on my chest and put the pack of
cigarettes on the headboard, then walked into the bathroom.

"I'm not gonna do anything with those", she said as she closed the
door.
I heard the water hit the bathtub a few seconds later, and pictured her
taking off her clothes and stepping in to the shower.
Then, as if she could read my thoughts, she opened the door slightly
and I watched her face peer through.

"We don't need the money"

Spring

I grew up here, in this forest.
All my friends are here, my family, my kin.
Weaker trees were planted here, and produced, but could not survive.
Often I would watch them grow, then suffer, then lose the battle for
survival and thriving.
I always felt I had a secret no one else had.
I knew a way that was smarter than the others, it was deeper, more
vast, and I had found this way and conquered the challenges of the
forest but upholding this inward decree of rebellion from what had
always been considered the way.
There was a time I was almost worshipped by the others.
There was a time some called me king.
But none could find the way I found.
None could live the life I've lived.
And they should never try.
The reality of my choices would frighten them.
So here I am:
Roots only inches deep
I've learned to survive on water falling to the surface
And sinking just below
They drank up every drop
But never begged for more
These roots found contention in my minimalism, but never fully being
able to grow and grasp the earth below.
I take only what I need to survive. Let the others thrive, and exhaust
themselves, and watch their fruit be plucked by every passerby who
wishes just to take what they've labored to grow. As for me, I'll give
when I choose to give, and receive when I need to receive, but I will
stand the test of time, my preservation is my priority, and I cannot be
destroyed.
Only now do I see the arrogance and sadness in that most "protected"
of stances.
But something has changed; something has shifted this tree to its core.

Another tree has been planted next to me.
A smaller, more fragile tree, but with strong branches and deeper,

though thinner roots.

"How does this work?" she asks me.

I'm struck silent by the innocence and purity in her voice, the apparent humility and desire in her tone.

Something of this briefest of encounters made me realize my method would not work for her as it's worked for me, and in this I began to wonder if it had ever really worked for me.

I bowed myself in shame, looking to the ground below.

"There's a much better place for you than here. Go deeper into the forest, there's nothing I can teach you that will help you."

"Well", she said, smiling. "All your fruit has been taken, so you must be doing something right."

In that moment I realized I had accomplished my goal, and this revelation was perhaps the most saddening.

I realized what was most important to me was not that my branches produced, but that they remained bare so I could not be taken advantage of, so I could not have to give to the hungry, to my neighbors and friends, to strangers.

I realized that after all these years of being planted here, all that mattered was that I appeared bare, as if I had already given all I had grown, and I have remained here just waiting for spring.

One can't see the roots from the surface, only their body can know their depth and length and strength.

But this quiet little tree just stood there, resilient and strong, though young and not as familiar with this forest.

She looked inside me, above me and below me, around me and through me. I could not show her what I've always shown the others. I could not speak to her the way I've spoken to the others. I would not lead her to places I've always taken the others. Something was too precious, something was too sincere and longing, the longing in her radiated and I felt the warmth from the moment we noticed each other.

Finally, I had to confess.

"I cannot help you, for I myself do not know the way."

Silence.

She looked around at the other trees, standing tall, strong, and shedding beautiful, colored leaves onto the grass and dirt below, then she looked back at me with a grace and love I had never expected to

see here.
"Then we will find the way together."

Plague

Sick with plague
I feel like Doc Holliday
I keep coughing
But keep smoking anyway
I've got my lady by my side
She collects my chips
When I'm out of time
We saddle up and head for richer land
I've raped this place
For gold and grace I
'm a king In the shell of a beggar
God knows I've played, and kept my fears at bay
I'm riding fast , straight out of the flames

...and if this will be my end... I'll go out...
Guns ablaze

The Strong Man

I've never been too good at being the strong man.
I struggle to control my cravings, and I fail at every attempt to hide
my emotions or their source.

Struggling hourly to control my appetites, I fear one day they will
consume me, as I have consumed them.
The truth is, I won't find anything on the Internet that will reign me
in, only pull me down into the well further.
I cannot understand my purpose. It is above me to comprehend.
And while I can recite to you or anyone else my meaning, to God, to
my employers, and to my loved ones and family, I deeply deny that
it's the truth.

I put everything off until tomorrow, because tomorrow I'll feel better.

Tomorrow I'll view the world as my playground, as a place where
anything is possible.
But today, today just isn't that day.
So I'll stare at the television, and spend the little money I do have on
wine and cigarettes, knowing that's the only way I'll get through the
night, knowing I'll be whole when I wake up tomorrow.
Sometimes I do things I know I'll regret, hoping that shame and fear
and regret will drive me tomorrow to become the man I want to
become. Perhaps it will motivate me to change, to grow, and to not be
afraid of my own passions and desires anymore.

Or maybe tomorrow, I'll just shut out the world and stare at naked
women on a computer screen.

Vitamins

I hate drinking water.
It makes me feel like I have to piss every five minutes.
I sit at my desk and drink coffee all day.
Sometimes, I'll put one of those vitamin C packets in the water, not for
the nutrition or to help boost my immune system, but because it takes
away from the taste of nothing that water is.
I'm prone to kidney stones, and I smoke too damn much.
But I still drink coffee all day, and I seem to smoke more when I'm
sick and coughing.
I pray for deliverance, for self-control and the will to change.
I pray for a new body, a renewed body.
Everyone tells me I have to quit, as if they believe I don't want to.
Maybe they know I'm weak.
Maybe they sit there, telling each other how little control I have over
my own impulses.
Maybe they laugh at how strong I make people believe I am, when in
reality, they know I'm powerless against my vices.
Maybe my weakness pushes them to be stronger themselves, and to
withstand temptation, as I am clearly unable to do.
Maybe they tell each other I'll get what I deserve, for not listening to
them, or to reason and common sense.
Or maybe they love me, and hope I'll live a very long time.

Glenoaks

I use a blank check as a bookmark.
My fear is that, one day, as I'm reading at a coffee shop
the wind will blow my check off the table
and down the street.
My fear is that someone will find it, and write a check for anything
less than $27,
wiping out my checking account in an instant.
It is this fear that will ultimately eclipse my good judgment
and send me running down Glenoaks Blvd after the check,
while the screenwriter at the table next to me looks up when I run off
and decides my Apple is newer and nicer than his Apple.
So he takes it and runs up Glenoaks Blvd in the opposite direction of
me.
Then, on my way back to the coffee shop,
once I've retrieved the check, and while I'm still a ways off
it will occur to me that my $2,000 laptop was left on the table.
I will rush back to make sure it's still there,
clutching my check and cursing to myself that running is the only
time I wish
I wasn't a smoker.
And as I'm crossing the street, and almost within view of my table,
a Metro bus will plow into my emaciated body at 52 miles per hour
and send my check flying into the air,
where someone-despite the tragic and gruesome scene before them-
will be
devious enough to snatch up the check and steal the pitiful amount of
money
in my account, which would have gone to my girlfriend after the bus
ended my sad run.
Luckily for the bus driver, I don't read at coffee shops.

Racists

I hate racists.

Rent Control

A city of angels.
I see them, standing outside the clubs
$15 parking
$25 cover (for guys, unless you walk in with six scantily clad
underage women)
$11 jack and cokes
The most paradoxical of "dress codes"
Enforced by huge dudes in light blue polo shirts
tucked into their black cargo pants
Their flesh colored earpieces plugged into walkie-talkies
Like they were guarding a government official or foreign dignitary

I see them, as I drive down Sunset on a Friday night, a plastic bag in
my lap
My own weekend entertainment awaits
A bottle of Mt Dew, a pack of Pall Mall's, and some ice cream
The pulsating beat fades in and out when he opens and closes the
door
I look out the window and watch as the rope is opened, closed,
opened, closed

We are so young.

Every billboard in town that isn't advertising a sequel
Is urging the population to get tested for HIV
I remember the scare
All three of them
Fear isn't as powerful a motivator as some exaggerate it to be
There's a fire inside some of us even the terror death and decay can't
extinguish
I can't help but think about this as I watch my generation
File slowly into a dark building
Dressed to kill
But my people will die a much slower death
We have to dance first
We have to buy the first round

Figure rent out on Sunday

"Ah, leave 'em alone", Frank says from the passenger seat. "We've all gotta make a few mistakes when we're young. It's part of growing up."

It's always made me uncomfortable
When people refer to children that way.

Rent Control

A city of angels.
I see them, standing outside the clubs
$15 parking
$25 cover (for guys, unless you walk in with six scantily clad
underage women)
$11 jack and cokes
The most paradoxical of "dress codes"
Enforced by huge dudes in light blue polo shirts
tucked into their black cargo pants
Their flesh colored earpieces plugged into walkie-talkies
Like they were guarding a government official or foreign dignitary

I see them, as I drive down Sunset on a Friday night, a plastic bag in
my lap
My own weekend entertainment awaits
A bottle of Mt Dew, a pack of Pall Mall's, and some ice cream
The pulsating beat fades in and out when he opens and closes the
door
I look out the window and watch as the rope is opened, closed,
opened, closed

We are so young.

Every billboard in town that isn't advertising a sequel
Is urging the population to get tested for HIV
I remember the scare
All three of them
Fear isn't as powerful a motivator as some exaggerate it to be
There's a fire inside some of us even the terror death and decay can't
extinguish
I can't help but think about this as I watch my generation
File slowly into a dark building
Dressed to kill
But my people will die a much slower death
We have to dance first
We have to buy the first round

Figure rent out on Sunday

"Ah, leave 'em alone", Frank says from the passenger seat. "We've all gotta make a few mistakes when we're young. It's part of growing up."

It's always made me uncomfortable
When people refer to children that way.

The Fountain of Youth

To hell with the fountain of youth
I fall on my knees
and place Your hands on my shoulders
And beg for a taste of forgiveness
And may it never leave my lips
Well into my declining years
May I never ask for more than this

It's hard to believe I was a child once
I never knew the difference between carefree and careless
And I never cared to know
The future was not a place I feared
But a distant country I longed to explore
Did I know You then?
Perhaps better than I know You now
Could I hear Your voice?
Somehow, I knew You were there
And as the years pass beneath me
I long to be born again

My insecurities cast a shadow that walks before me
My innocence has faded away
I find myself in that distant country
Just trying to make my way back home
Then you wake up one cold November morning
And realize you're a bitter old man
And you're not even an old man
And you've never even been to war
And you've never even fought to keep everything you've spent your
whole life earning
And you hate yourself for no other reason than the fact that time has
caught up with you
And the only proof of this inward despair is the emptiness of my
language

And I've hurt myself once more

From throwing the anchor over the side of this ship
Yet, once anchored, the waves crash into me
And break me
And test me
But when these waves wash over me
How clean I am
And free, and ready to sail...if only I had learned to sail
Like my father before me
And his father before him.

To hell with the fountain of youth
I fall on my knees
and place Your hands on my shoulders
And beg for a taste of forgiveness
May it never leave my lips
Well into my declining years
May I never ask for more than this

Burn or Bury

Sitting below an opium cloud
Midnight was yesterday
No one ever kills a man for fame

Her hand touches my hand
Walking down the hallway again
I've never felt more like less of a man

Numb from the day he was born
Calloused, fucking, cursing, running
Turned around when I saw his shadow
But I drew first this time

Two in the chest, one in the throat
Watch the blood pour through his fingers
As he grips the wound
And I want to feel sorry
But he always was a fool

Burn or bury
Twenty-nine Hail Mary's
And I'm free.

A Good Knight's Sleep

The streets are dead
As the fog rolls in
It's a Monday on Highway 99
There's blood and sweat
On a broken fence
My eyes are bruised and my knuckles are red

I climb through the window
And under your bed
Where I found your paintings
And letters you sent
And the letter read…

Where'd you go?
What did you do?
Why did you have to disappear into the night?
It's the longest kiss goodbye

This whole night started with a gunshot
One shot of Jack with a letter attached that read:
Ignorance is why you fear the night.
But I'm only afraid
When I've got the right things to say
I pull down the shoebox, dust it, and open the lid
And the letter read…

Where'd you go?
What did you do?
Why did you have to disappear into the night?
It's the longest kiss goodbye

I've been alone a year or two
I get by cause I have to
And when I leave you, you'll know why
It's always the longest kiss goodbye

I saw your face and a picture of love
I'm falling from grace and you're lifting me up

The Wine

Tommy Barlowe, relieved of his sorrow
There's blood on the road where he died
Molly followed, with pills that she swallowed
Their love drove the light from their eyes

Frayed by all this, yet children of promise
There's breath in the tears that they've cried
Never fathered, but never to wander
They drank from the well of our lies

We fled our towers
Our kings and our cowards
We roamed through the desert and night
A search for water, the claim of our father
The land where we'll bury our crimes

Why'd you have to pass this cup to me?
You said the wine would stand the test of time
And chains will lose their hold
I believe in every word you ever spoke
But thirty years inside this flesh and bones
I'm holding on to holding on to
Know

A Psalm for Those

It began as a whisper
Before I could imagine what would have happened
Had I not been listening...
I heard it:

"Come out here..."

The weeks struck and passed like lighting flashes
On the sea, in the night
Each one further from the other
Unpredictable
Momentary
Silent

"The light shines in the darkness...but the darkness can not
comprehend it"
And I cannot comprehend the light
Nor the darkness
And I'm sitting in the silence in between
Waiting for the word
Whether it comes by whisper or by thunder
My sails will rise
And my oars will find their stride
But for now, I'm waiting for the word

But this night the ship was beaten and compromised
Tossing back and forth as the water leapt onto the deck
And all became fragile enough for me to know
We were sinking
I grabbed the chain from its post and began to pull
Faster and faster, the rain pounding against my face
The metal burning my skin as I gripped it and pulled
Until I could pull it no further
I ran to the side of the ship and looked down into the black, raging
sea
The anchor was steadfast, and there was no one to help me

I pounded my hands on the wood and shouted into the night sky
"Where are you?"
I went below the deck
Where I sleep but never rest
Where I wake but never awaken
I pulled all the drawers from the cabinet
As the light above my table swung back and forth in the storm

The needle was broken and I had thrown all the pills overboard
The bottle was empty and I had put your letters in its place

I sank to the floor
Almost drowning though no water filled my room
But I couldn't stay here
No
I'm not going down like this
Not now

I rushed back up the stairs and onto the deck
Pacing back and forth, lantern in hand
Searching for a sign
A signal
A beacon
A light
When I realized...

The storm I thought was raging against my vessel
Was your waves washing over me
The figure I saw dancing on the water
Was not my end, but my beginning
The whisper I feared was my adversary
Was the deep calling unto deep

...and it began as a whisper
Before I could imagine what would have happened
Had I not been listening...
I heard it:

"Come out here…"

Flares

The fire truck broke down on the railroad tracks
I was late for work and my light turned green
A dozen or so cars lined up behind me
No time to keep watching my rear view mirror
I wondered about the truck's fate all day as I sat at my desk
Realizing the last hour of my life passed by uneventfully
And the few dollars I made in that hour
Will pay for my lunch sometime next week
Tom chased after the girl who came crying out of the elevator
And he never returned to work after that
Maybe he caught up with her.
Maybe when he did, they fell in love.
Maybe he's more content with love and a poor life than having a
pocket full of cash for the week and dying slowly staring at a series of
worksheets on a computer, getting by.
I didn't know Tom that well, but I admire him now. We talk about
him over coffee in the mornings. We dream up our various stories of
what must have happened to him after that day.
Jeffrey thinks they eloped to Las Vegas before moving to Europe,
taking labor jobs and living in a flat somewhere.
No matter where he is, Tom has been immortalized in the sequestered
imaginations of a few employees here.
When I got downstairs and into my car at the end of the shift, I
rubbed my eyes, trying to shake off the digitizing of the past 9 hours.
As I pulled out of the parking lot and onto Victory Blvd, I saw no
debris on the ground near the tracks
No caution tape
No burned out road flares
Or news vans and cameras
And for some reason, my heart was sad
Not because it hoped for tragedy
I guess I was just looking for a disruption of the order we all work so
hard to uphold.
I made my way up the hill toward my house in the dark
And wondered how Tom and that girl from the elevator were going
to spend Christmas Eve.

If the Medicine Fails

If love is flying kites near the Santa Monica pier
And talking the sun out of hiding
The dull ache when you're away
Or when I'm too sick to see you
Then love is alright
If the fear sets in when your voice is shaking
If I can't feel you when I really want to feel you
Then we can call it love
and that would be alright
If I hurt you
Without you having to tell me I hurt you
And I make amends before you ask me to
Then perhaps love is alright
They say it will "stand the test of time"
But time is not a test
It is a gift
One we must protect
We must fight for its honor
Uphold its value
We must own it, not be owned by it
We are not slaves to time
We ride it like a wave
Then swim out
And ride again

And should some sickness overtake you
If the medicine fails
Then we will pray
Closing my hands over your hands
And pressing them together
We will pray
And if the hospital chair is too stiff to sleep in
Then I will crawl into the bed with you and sleep by your side
Waking when you wake
Resting only after you're long asleep

And if you are forever in good health
Then let's welcome each day
With thankfulness
I promise to never take advantage of a smile
To never take advantage of the suns warmth
Breaking through the curtains into our room
And waking me before you
So I can prepare your day
So I'll be there when your first conscious breath is taken
When your first movement of the day is to put your hand on my face
And whisper, "Go away", and smile
I will go away
and smile

If love is my intimate obsession with
The way your eyes remain closed after we kiss
And the way you pull on my shirt
Throwing a still mourn across the room when I have to go to work
Then the glowing smile because you know when I'm returning
Then love is alright

And if God should bless us with a boy
I pray he has his mothers smile
Her hunger and thirst for truth
Her unparalleled and irreversible craving for life to be more than a
series of days running together and drowned in the meaningless
frivolity of just existing
I pray the child has her warmth
The compassion she carries like a satchel of medicine, waiting to be
dispersed among the castaways of the world

And if he should have anything of mine
I pray it is the love I bear for his mother
So he can know what I know
And the common ground he and I will always share
Is the awe we spend our lives, our words, and our songs trying to
somehow express to our God

If this is love

Then everything will be alright.

About the Author

Brian Wayne Foster is an American writer, poet, singer, and storyteller. Brian was born in Long Beach and raised in Southern California and the Central Valley. He began writing poetry and short stories at 12 years old, and began playing music at age 15. He performed in various theatrical productions and bands throughout high school and his early twenties, before returning to Los Angeles in 2008. He has been a student of theology and the human condition for the past decade, and his writings reflect the inner conflict of these two sets of ideas. Brian's first collection of writings, "Blackened White," released in April of 2012, and was on the Amazon Best Seller list within 2 days. His first EP of original songs "Odessa" released in March of 2013. Brian currently lives in Hollywood, CA.
Parking sucks.

Made in the USA
Middletown, DE
02 January 2021